For More Information or to Contact the Author: kpcp84@aol.com

ISBN 978-0-578-24475-4

Cover Image of Rainbow:
Courtesy clipartkey.com

Cover Image of Cupcake:
© Ahmad Safarudin | Dreamstime.com

Cover Design & Contents Layout: KJP Creatives

Printed in the United States of America by:
48HrBooks, 2249 14th St. SW, Akron, OH 44314

Pink Cupcakes & Rainbows

Short Stories From the Fight Against
the Monster We Call Cancer

Cheri Palmer-
Pannebaker

DEDICATION

*I want to dedicate this to Morgan
who told me to "write the book" ~
and to all those who are finding their way
in this big crazy world.
I want to call back to you and tell you that
I know for sure God is the real deal,
and it's safe for you to trust Him.*

*He will never leave you,
He will never forsake you ~
no matter what your "monster" is!!*

*In Loving Memory of
Dean ~ Duane ~ Pastor Griffith
True warriors in their fight and in their faith.
We will see you again!*

CONTENTS

CONTENTS

FOREWARD

Sometimes it still seems incomprehensible to me that two of the four children in our family have been diagnosed with cancer. Brad was 39 and Cheri was 54 when each received the devastating news. Cancer is such a brutal diagnosis and yet for our family, their stories have not just been about a nasty disease, but about the grace of a wonderful God. I really think you should hear more of the story.

I was riding in my truck with our Dad the day that Brad received his cancer diagnosis. Dad was talking to Brad on the phone and he made a statement that my brother and I both heard and never forgot. Dad said, "Just remember that when life is at its worst, God is at His best". For Brad, life soon became worse than it had ever been. For months, the cancer waged a war in Brad's body that sometimes seemed overwhelming. Together as a family, we rallied around him for the fight of his life – which amazingly he won. As a thrilling testimony of God's grace, Brad made God look really good even when life was really bad. In a whole new way, I came to understand what it truly means to glorify God. Five years later he would complete an Ironman Triathlon to celebrate that he was cancer-free.

None of us could have imagined that within a few years, another one of our siblings would also receive the heartbreaking diagnosis of cancer. While away from home, caring for a newborn granddaughter, Cheri discovered the first indicator that something was wrong. Suddenly the journey started all over again.

The Cancer Institute at Hershey Medical Center became like a second home. Doctor's appointments, scans, surgical procedures, chemotherapy, and radiation all became chapters in Cheri's story. My wife Patty and I became family companions and caregivers for Cheri and Kevin. We cried together during the hard times, and we celebrated together during the good times. Cancer came and went, and came and went again. Stage 4 cancer that metastasized basically created a lifelong journey for my sister that will never end until this life is over. Yet one thing is obvious. I have now been allowed to watch Cheri, just as Brad did, glorify God by making God look really good when life was really bad. Her testimony for the Lord has already touched a multitude of lives. Of course, there have been all the human responses of discouragement, disillusionment, doubt, and even despair. Yet through every moment of the last three years, there has still been God. God was there to give strength in moments of weakness, direction in times of uncertainty, peace in periods of turmoil, courage during outbursts of fear, and above all grace, His grace, sufficient grace, when Cheri needed it the most.

So, in reality, I guess this really is not my sister's story. It certainly is not just another book about cancer. It is not even a great praise of doctors and medical facilities that have marvelously cared for her. This book is a collection of stories about God. I have always defined God's providence as "the hand of God that is writing the story of my life". As you read these pages, you will see the hand of God over and over again. Cheri did not make this journey alone. She did not write this story by herself. She did not deal with a potentially terminal illness just because she had a strong will and a positive attitude. Her story is a "God story" and as you read it you will be amazed at the ways that God's grace was sufficient, and that God was glorified.

My dear sister, I truly do love you. Thank you for allowing me to be a part of your story. I can also honestly say that I really love God as well. Could it be that both of those statements are true – because of cancer? They are. Absolutely!

Tom Palmer

INTRODUCTION

Several months before my diagnosis I started thinking about what I wanted to do with my life now that all my kids were grown and married. I started praying about it ~ telling the Lord I would love to do something for others whether it was volunteering at a hospital in some way or being an errand girl for elderly folks and shut-ins. I really didn't care if it was something I would get paid to do ~ just wanted to do more with my life.

It wasn't too long after my talks with Him that I was diagnosed with cancer. Trust me ~ that was NOT what I had in mind when I would ask Him what He wanted me to do with the years I still had here on this earth.

I had a few more good talks with the Lord, and I told Him that if He was allowing this in my life I wanted Him to look good in the yuck and the cruel and the ugly. I also told Him that now would be a good time for Him to show me that all the promises I had been taught and memorized and believed were true. I told the Lord that if He showed up for me ~ I would spend the rest of my life telling everyone around me that for sure, He is real...that He does keep His promises...that He can be trusted...that He's a good God even when the circumstances are not.

And so here we are ~ He has kept His end of the deal, and now it is my turn to do what I promised Him that I would do. That is why I am writing this book.

I pray that as you read these little stories you will be thrilled by the ways He showed up ~ how He carried me ~ how He worked out so many details ~ how He had treasures and treats all along the way to remind me He was right there and using many of you to let me know that.

There will be some tear jerkers...there will be some funnies...there will be complete honesty...and there will be stories that make us all realize how amazing our God is!!

I want to tell these stories as if you were just sitting in my home with me and we were talking. I am not fancy. I might not always get everything perfect in my wording and such ~ but it will just be me ~ talking to you ~ telling of His goodness and grace.

Cheri Palmer-Pannebaker

I love to tell the story

Of unseen things above,

Of Jesus and His glory,

Of Jesus and His love.

I love to tell the story,

Because I know it's true,

It satisfies my longings

As nothing else can do.

I love to tell the story,

'Twill be my theme in glory

To tell the old, old story

Of Jesus and His love.

I Love to Tell the Story (Public Domain)
By: Kate Hankey & William G. Fischer

Two Impacts

Yes, it took God two times to get my attention and to help me realize there was something wrong in my body.

I was going along just fine ~ feeling healthy and strong. I was enjoying life with my husband, Kevin, and my kids and their families. Baseball...parties...shopping... picnics...all that good stuff!!

One morning I started upstairs to grab something and I ran into the banister at the bottom of the stairs. It didn't feel too good but I didn't think much of it and went right on. A week or so later the exact same thing happened.

During that next week I noticed some bruising and my first thought was that it must be from running into the banister two times in a row. I mentioned it to my mother and to Kevin and we all agreed that most likely that was the case. Because our newest granddaughter was to be born in the next week or so we decided I should just focus on that and if things got worse I would have it checked when we got back from meeting the baby.

Little did I know then that God was already working and was doing what He could to help me find something that had gone undetected and unnoticed.

How creative was He??!!

Angel
Straight From
Heaven

It was time to head to Indiana. Our son, Kyle, and his wife Kelly's baby was to be born that Saturday. I could hardly think straight from the excitement as we packed our bags. I did my best to never see the bruising and to block it out of my mind. After all, I had a baby to meet and I didn't have time for bruises and scary things.

Lowyn Jade Pannebaker was born in the wee hours Sunday morning. We got to meet the perfect little doll later that morning and once again life had changed forever. There was a new member in our family and we were in love.

Kevin and I had only planned to stay for a couple days but Monday morning Kyle and Kelly asked if I would stay for the whole week. Kevin would go back to PA and work and then come back to get me the following weekend. Offer me time with a baby and I would be perfectly happy to wear the same clothes over and over for a week.

The little and her mommy came home from the

hospital mid-week. I didn't think I could be any happier. They let her sleep in my room at night. I got to rock and cuddle her during the day as much as I wanted.

One morning I jumped out of bed to go find Kelly and see if she needed me for anything. I was hurrying to get dressed and the street light was shining in my room and I caught a glimpse of a lump with the bruising. I FROZE!! The whole world stood still in that moment. I had cotton mouth. I felt dizzy and almost like I was on the outside looking in on that moment.

I was shaking as I ran to find Kelly at the other end of the house. I told her that I thought I saw a tumor. I finally touched it and it felt like a rock. I think Kelly and I both knew that something was very wrong and that in another way our lives were changing forever.

Now God in His great wisdom knew that the thing I love most on this earth is a baby. How gracious of Him to allow me to find something so terrifying when I could be handed a baby to calm my shaking nerves and soothe my terrified feelings. Kevin would not be back for a couple more days and I honestly believe that God gave me those days to ease the blow and to help me somehow wrap my brain around what most likely was ahead of me.

Lowyn continued to stay in my room at night. She

would have her nighttime feeding and then I would sit in Kyle's desk chair and rock her long past the time that she was already back to sleep.

I would pray and pray that God would be willing to let me be ok, and to be able to live, and to watch this little girl that I was madly in love with grow older.

Weeks before I had picked a lullaby just for her that I had wanted to sing to her when I would rock her.

Some of the words to that song are ~

"And you'll never know how much I love you,
But I'll keep on telling you my whole life thru.
Now I believe in miracles and you're the reason why.
So dream on while I sing you my angel lullaby."

I never could sing it to her...I cried too hard each time. It wouldn't be till many months later that I would be able to sing it to her for the first time.

God gave me a priceless gift those nights. I laid her right where the tumor was and I held her tight. Only God knows, and saw the number of tears that dripped on her precious head. I would tell her that she truly was an angel. Sent to us just when Amma was gonna need the extra courage and motivation to fight a monster that was bigger than any of us could imagine.

Perfect
Timing

Kevin came back to Indiana on Saturday. That afternoon he took a lot of black and white photos of me with Lowyn. I held her through her naps that day knowing that in the morning we would drive away.

Sunday morning we said our goodbyes. I held Lowyn one last time and soaked in the sweet smell of a newborn and kissed her warm soft skin over and over ~ almost as if I was absorbing her to help me in the days to come. All I could do then was lay her down and run to the car and not look back.

Monday morning I got up dreading what I knew I had to do. Before I had gotten home I had asked our daughter, Krista, to check with one of her friends who was a nurse and see who she would recommend I should ask for at the Women's Health Center. She suggested the best doctor, and said that she was very hard to get in with, but I could at least ask for her.

I told the Lord I would call the office at ten o'clock that morning, but until then I was going to go about my normal routine of fixing tea and eating some cereal and starting a load of laundry. It gave me a sense of control to set a time and make that decision on my own, and it gave the Lord some time to work out the details exactly how He wanted them to go.

Ten o'clock came way too soon. I got out the phone number and sat down and dialed. I'm not sure I was breathing at the time. I got a wonderful person on the other end and I explained my situation. I told her a friend recommended a certain doctor. She said she was the very best, and believe it or not just five minutes before I called she had gotten a cancellation and said I could have that spot. Ok, WOW!!! Now if that is not God doing His thing I don't know what it would be!!! The appointment wouldn't be till Wednesday which gave me a couple of days to unpack and rest, and somehow find the way to get myself to that appointment.

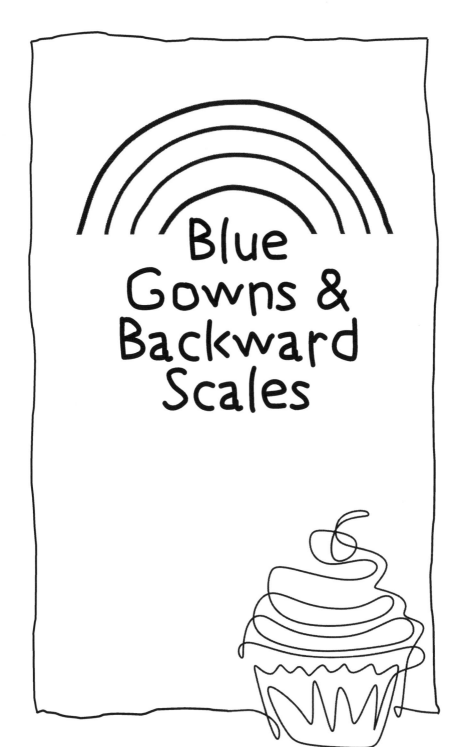

Blue Gowns &
Gowns &
Backward
Scales

It seems ironic now that the thing I hated most in life
was hospitals and doctor appointments and most anything
medical related. I was just beginning a journey where the
medical world would become my way of life for many years
to come.

As Wednesday arrived, the two things I dreaded most
were the skimpy gowns that they make you put on and I did
NOT want to get weighed.

Once again God had it covered. The sweetest nurse
took me back to my room, and Krista had told me before I
went to stand backwards on the scale so I didn't have to see
my weight. BRILLIANT!! For all I knew I was as skinny as I
was when I first got married. I mean I could at least think
that I was.

Then it was time for the lovely gowns ~ which turned
out to be lovely!! The nurse handed me a soft navy blue
gown that covered me from head to toe. So far so good!!

God was taking care of all my little worries and concerns, knowing full well that I would need everything else I had, to deal with what was coming next.

The doctor came in and within minutes I understood why she was considered the best. She was the perfect doctor for me. Gentle. Kind. Soft spoken. A listener. She asked me a lot of questions and I told her the whole story. She then examined me and within just a couple of minutes she started ordering all kinds of tests.

Before she left the room she told me that she would be completely honest with me, and that it was not a cyst or just a bad bruise ~ although running into the banister had created a very serious bruise. There was a large pocket of blood which was what drew my attention to it. Ultimately leading me to see a doctor and she was able to confirm there was a tumor.

I often think how amazing it is to be loved and cared for by a God that was so committed to me that He forced me to find something I probably would have missed for a long time yet. I was so busy with life that it would have been easy to not even think of going for a checkup, because I felt great and wasn't aware of any reason for concern.

When I was done with the doctor I went to the checkout desk to schedule all the tests that were ordered.

I already knew then in my heart that I had cancer, and yet somehow there was a peace and calmness that I could never explain. I always thought that if I was told I had cancer I would probably lose my mind and not be able to function. Instead I stood there and took care of what I needed to. I looked across the room and mouthed to Kevin that it was not good, but that I was ok. That is the peace of God that is beyond our understanding and that peace was going to visit me multitudes of times in the years to come.

Tests, Tests & More Tests

First there was a mammogram. Second there was an ultrasound. Then there would be an ultrasound guided biopsy. I was already over it and ready to be done with it all, but we were in head first now and there was no turning back. The day came for the biopsy. Just the word causes a feeling of anxiety. Not to mention not knowing what all would be done. Would it be painful?? I was to be awake. Would I just freak out?? Have a panic attack?? Cry??

I had two wonderful nurses that got everything set up. The room was darkened and cool and I did like the hum of all the machines. The whole ceiling was painted with flowers. I tried to focus on the flowers while they did all the things they needed to do to get ready for the doctor who would do the biopsy.

The nurses were doing some ultrasounds and I heard them say "there's one...oh there's another one. Yes, that is one too". Um, that is when the anticipated panic set in. I honestly thought they were finding tumors. Imagine my relief when they told me they were locating lymph nodes because they were going to test some of those too.

Before too much longer the doctor came in and he was just as kind and nice as the nurses were. I caught a glimpse of a needle that looked like the size of a knitting needle and I decided it was best for me to keep my eyes focused on the flowers on the ceiling, and think about the One that created them, and who was with me that very moment giving me courage and grace.

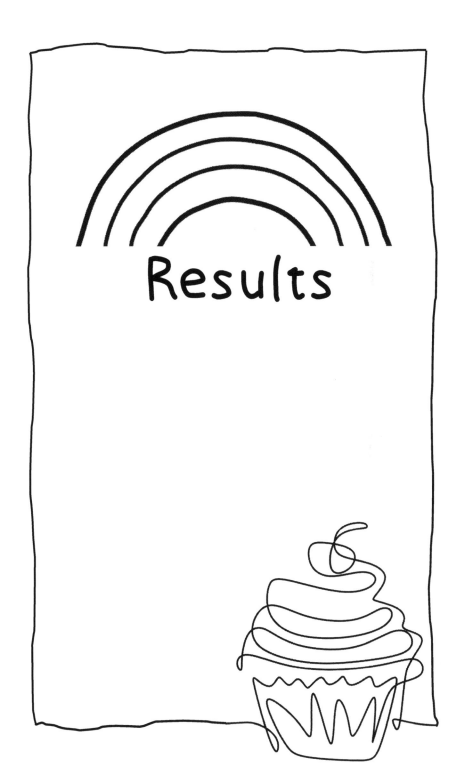

Results

It took about a week before I got the final results. I very much remember just going about my everyday life. I slept well at night. I ate well. I felt good. I don't remember being afraid. I kept very busy and did things that I loved to do.

"All my days were written in your book and planned before a single one of them began." Ps. 139:16

"The life of every living thing is in His hand, as well as the breath of all mankind." Job 12:10

Long before I was ever born, God knew that on October 5, 2017 at 11 o'clock in the morning, I would get that call that would change the rest of my life one way or another. Yes, I did indeed have cancer. Yes, it broke my heart.

I called Kevin...I called my parents...I told my kids...and the rest of my family and closest friends. I think I was numb with a grace God gives for such times as this.

I had no doubt in my mind that I would be here on this earth for the exact number of days that God had already planned for me to be here. I knew that He would either heal me on this earth or heal me in His presence. Either way, I knew I could pray for complete healing with the confidence that He would. I just prayed He would be willing to do it here on this earth so I could have more time with my family.

I determined that day that I would do everything possible to fight for life. I had zero clue what was ahead of me. It's a good thing God doesn't let us know too much in advance. I was only going to have grace for one thing at a time.

During those few days that I had to wrap my brain around this new reality, I read this thought in a beautiful coffee table book our niece, Julie, had already sent to me weeks before...

And if not...HE IS STILL GOOD

God was still going to be a good God...simply by definition...by character. A good, good God even when life was not.

Rainbows

I'm going to tell you a couple of stories as to why rainbows became so special to me.

After all my tests and results were done in Lebanon, I was then referred to Hershey Medical Center for all my future care. I had a bunch of new appointments made with them, but I had a week or two break. I told Kevin I needed to make one more quick trip to Indiana so see Kyle's family before I got into the heart of the treatment and wouldn't be able to make trips for a long time.

By then Lowyn was about a month old. She could smile. She slept in our room each night. We cuddled thru naps. The weekend flew by. Sunday morning I wrote a note and put it on their fridge that said I WOULD BE BACK SOME-DAY!!!!!! I didn't have any clue if I was even going to live, or how long I would have to fight hard...but I was going to see them again!!!!!!

We headed east and it seemed I could not stop the

constant flow of tears that dripped onto my lap. It's hard enough to say goodbye to your kids and a baby let alone when you know you are going home to fight cancer.

We were riding along in silence. My brain felt numb. And literally out of the clear blue a brilliant rainbow appeared right in front of our car. Of course it was up in the sky ~ but literally right ahead of us, and as clear as day!!! Now there wasn't any rain or any reason for a rainbow. The sky was blue. The sun was brilliant. And yet there it was. Kevin saw it too and we were both stunned.

As we drove past, this overwhelming sense of peace came over me. I felt that God just wanted us to see that to remind us of His promises. To let me know that when I got back that evening and had to start more hard tests and procedures in Hershey, He was going to be right there with me.

The other amazing rainbow was when we were at Niagara Falls about a year later and we had taken a walk down to the water. Hundreds of people were everywhere. It was cloudy and so it was not the best formula for making a rainbow off the falls. I quietly prayed that God would somehow let me see a rainbow. It honestly was not more than a few seconds later and the sun came out from behind a cloud and the most magnificent rainbow draped over the falls. In that moment hundreds of people were taking pictures and admiring God's creation and giving Him glory whether they realized it or not. Under my breath I told them they were all welcome. Haha!! God had sent that for me, but I was glad they could enjoy it too.

By now I was starting to realize I was in over my head...that I had a rough road ahead of me! I had gone to Hershey for some tests and procedures because they wanted their own records from their own technicians and equipment.

The worst thing I had to endure was an MRI guided biopsy that went all wrong. I was face down with my arms strapped behind me. My legs strapped together. I had to put my face down in a mold. And then they put me in the MRI machine over and over as they tried to get some of my flesh to do their own biopsy. My tears literally dropped out of the mold and down onto the floor. It took over three hours. I was so dizzy and weak from the position I was in, and not having been able to eat, and the constant motion of the machine going in and out of the tunnel. At one point I pushed the buzzer they gave me, and they helped me sit up and I told them I was done. I sat there and cried. They begged me to try one more time. Somehow I dug real deep and I suppose an extra dose of grace came in that room. I told them that they had one more chance and then I was leaving. Thank the good Lord that within a few minutes they finally had what they needed. They pulled me out of the tunnel again and as I sat up they handed me my glasses and I could see drops of my blood on the floor. It felt inhuman. I was pretty sure I was not made for such things and maybe I just needed to tap out.

I couldn't even talk about it for a few days. I would just tell Kevin that it was horrid and I was too broken and sad to even tell him what happened. Finally, one day I was able to tell my mother and she cried with me.

One night I gave in and said this word to Kevin ~ "whyyyyyyyyyyyyyyyy???" What had I ever done to deserve this?? I told him that I had always tried to obey those in authority over me...always tried to do what God asked us to do in obedience to Him. I was a faithful wife and mother. And I looked around at others that weren't even trying half the time and their lives were great!!

This is the quote Mr. Honey read to me that night from J. D. Walt ~

"Trouble is the unfortunate feature and a bitter fruit of the insanely complex, compounded brokenness of a whole fallen creation. It is neither an indictment on the goodness of God, nor the faith of His followers."

In other words...bad things do happen to good people. In this world we were promised that we would have trouble. We were also promised that God would provide all we need for every need we have. I wasn't necessarily being punished for something or less loved by God. It could easily just be because we live in a broken, fallen, imperfect world.

Pink
Cupcakes

I found the courage to move forward. I finished all the extra appointments and the tests that they had ordered. The next thing on the list would be to go to the breast center and meet my surgeon, and she would go over everything and decide if I would have surgery first or chemo first.

The breast center was just down the hall from where I had been getting some tests done. As I was leaving for the last time before I would come back to the breast center, I mentioned to Kevin that maybe I could just go down the hall and peek in. Welllllll, much to my surprise everyone was wearing pink t-shirts. There were pink cupcakes and other refreshments. People were smiling and talking. It looked like a rather happy place. It sure looked much less scary than I had imagined.

It was now the day for my big appointment. My younger brothers ~ Brad and Scott ~ had been visiting my folks, and before they were gonna head back to Arkansas they said they wanted to meet Kevin and me there. They were hoping that maybe they could meet my surgeon and just see where I would be and such.

Much to my dismay, when we arrived at the breast center there were no pink cupcakes!!!! WHAT??!!! I asked the girls at the check in desk where the pink cupcakes were and they told me that was just a special thing they had done for breast cancer awareness month. Ahhhhhhh!!!

Everyone was so wonderful and helpful and kind ~ from the girls at the front desk to the nurses. Brad and Scott sat in the waiting room with their pink t-shirts on while Kevin and I went back for meetings. I met my surgeon ~ Dr. Paulishak ~ and she was once again the perfect doctor for me. Gentle and soft spoken and kind. We had a good meeting and she decided that for me, we would do chemo first and then have my surgery later. I hugged her because I'm a hugger and then I asked if she would be kind enough to come meet my brothers. She was so gracious and came out to the waiting room and talked with them for a little bit. Both of my brothers told me later that they could not have hand picked a better person to be my surgeon and they were thrilled that she would be on my team of doctors.

Back to the lack of pink cupcakes!! While I was in my meetings, Brad and Scott went over to Chocolate World and

they asked someone that worked there if they would decorate a cupcake for me in pink. Sure enough she did and they
had brought it back for me so I would have my pink cupcake
~ just like the ones that had made me smile a couple weeks
before.

Thank you dear Brad and Scott for coming that day ~
for being a part of the journey I was on ~ for letting me
know I would not be alone. THANK YOU for my cupcake. I
will never forget that!!!!!! I love you both forever. I am beyond blessed to have three brothers that I consider some of
my best friends. I know for a fact that each one of them will
always walk alongside me in this fight!!

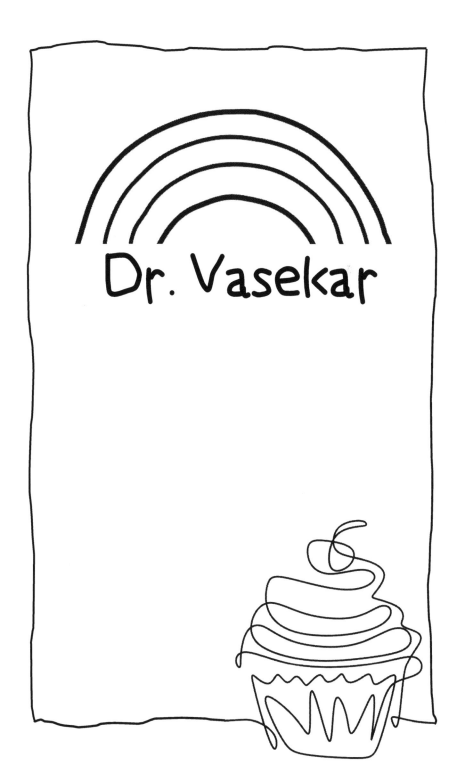

Dr. Vasekar

I am pretty sure that none of us could ever imagine that someday we would be going to the cancer institute of a hospital for an appointment. I'm very sure that all of us hope that is never the case for ourselves or anyone we know and love.

My day had come. I got up and went about my normal morning routine as if life was somehow normal. I had looked up my oncologist online and she looked so sweet and I was pretty sure I would feel comfortable with her. She also was highly rated as an outstanding doctor and that was a huge encouragement!!

Kevin came and picked me up and we rode in silence. I don't think we even know how to process moments like that as humans. It almost seemed like it was a movie I was watching or somehow was in but it wasn't real.

We pulled up to the front of the beautiful Cancer Institute and someone took our car. Valet parking is provided for cancer patients which is pretty classy. As the months would go by, I would find out how important it was to be dropped off right at the door of the hospital, and to have Kevin with me while someone else took our car and parked it.

First thing inside the door you register for your appointments. I still felt like it wasn't real. I had a wonderful check in assistant and she made me feel important and she genuinely cared and said she would be thinking about me as I began this huge fight.

I was sent to the second floor and there was a big waiting room with lots of people in it. I was given a clipboard and I had to fill out the same forms and answer the same questions I had done over and over and over again for months.

As I sat there with my pen, I began to feel my whole jaw quiver. Big tears ran down my face and dripped off my chin and onto my shirt. I answered "no" to every question except one...do you have cancer?? I didn't have another thing wrong with me but I had cancer. The one big deadly monster that everyone dreaded.

I finished my paperwork and then I looked around the room. All I kept thinking was I do not belong here. I do not belong here. I want to go home. This is not my life. This is a mistake. More tears ran and then it hit me ~ no one else belonged there either. None of us signed up for this. We all had other things we needed and wanted to be doing. And yet there we sat...all sharing one thing in common...cancer.

I finally got to meet Dr. Vasekar. Once again God had blessed me with the perfect doctor for me. We went over many things and we set the plans for my future in motion. We made an agreement that day that we would always be honest with each other. That we would never push my body to a place where there was no quality of life. Quality of life would always come first rather than just keeping me alive for a quantity of days.

Dr. Vasekar ~ you are not only my amazing oncologist but you are my friend. Thank you for respecting me. Thank you for listening to me. Thank you for hearing me. Thank you for making me feel like part of the team as we all work together. You are a joy and a blessing to me. I love you and I will be grateful for you forever!!!!!!

The
Four Littles

The two things I dreaded most about having cancer were having to eventually tell the four older grandkids and losing all my hair. We had been able to keep it from the kids for months while I went through all the preliminary appointments and procedures. By now, the number was up to 14 of those appointments and procedures.

I didn't want the grands to see me any differently than just their Amma. Not as a cancer patient. Not as a sick person. Not as someone who might be dying soon. Just Amma!!! At that time in life we did everything together. Target runs. Grocery shopping. Playgrounds. Even a dreadful farm show trip!!!! I didn't want anything to change...I didn't want to change...I didn't want our relationships to change.

Our daughter, Krista, handled it perfectly one morning. Just the honest simple truth. Before lunch there was a knock on the door and they had brought lunch to me and had each colored a picture for me. They were a little sheepish and I realized that the key would be for me to act as normal as possible and put them at ease. They had a lot of questions and I answered honestly. Mostly they just wanted to be together and do kids stuff and that was perfect for me.

Later I read their notes ~

"I hope you get better soon. I am praying for you."

"Amma, I hope you don't die."

Well God bless them. It was just one of those raw, painful moments that come with all of this, and all I could think was that I hope I don't die either. I was only 54 years old. My brain could not even comprehend ever leaving this earth period. Let alone leaving my babies...five of them at that time.

Sustaining Grace

I love the words...and i love this definition that we
have heard John Piper say before ~

*"Not grace to bar what is not bliss...nor flight from all
distress but this...the grace that orders our trouble and pain
and then in the darkness is there to sustain."*

Over and over again God has not spared me from the
pain and the struggle and the hurt and the sadness buttttt
He has always sustained me. Has been there to carry me
through. And sometimes with extra treats along the way
like the following.

I had finally sat down and faced something I kept
putting off. But I knew I needed to be prepared for when my
hair all fell out in a few weeks. So I went online and found
some scarves and hats I liked and got an order together. I
couldn't even begin to imagine myself bald...or imagine how

I would look in these things. As happened so often the tears came. I didn't want to do this. I didn't want to be bald or sick. I sure didn't want to die. I wanted to walk away from the computer and make it all go away. Before I could even complete the order a package was dropped off on my porch, so in the excitement to see what that was I quickly clicked 'submit order' and closed the computer.

I opened the front door to find a luxurious gift from my friend, Gretchen. It was from the Ritz Carlton Spa. There was a white robe...white slippers...all kinds of samples of soaps and lotions and shampoos, and the most amazing candle I have ever burned to this day.

Now that's what I call sustaining grace. He didn't take away the fact that I was going to go bald...He didn't take away the fact that I needed to order things to cover my bald head...buttttt He graciously showered me with love and care, thru a dear friend, at just the moment I needed to forget all the sad stuff and feel happy and grateful and loved.

Sustaining Grace ~ probably one of the most profound things to me in this whole experience!!!!

Chemo ~ Round One

It's pretty scary to sit and sign papers that say that I understand that the drugs themselves could take my life.

It was time for the first round of six. The nurses all called it the "red devil" of chemo because what I was getting was so strong. I would get one bag of anti- nausea medication and then four different bags of chemo drugs. It would take probably five or six hours each time.

My brother, Tom, and his wife, Patty, came to be with us that day. I had my blood drawn thru my port which had been placed less than two weeks prior. My port was also accessed then to allow all the bags of drugs to go into my body.

I was finally taken back to my infusion room and Patty was with me at the time and Kevin and Tom were out in the lobby working and reading. My nurse hooked up the anti-nausea bag and she told me that if I started to feel funny to let her know right away. She said that just in the past week she had had several patients have an allergic reaction. I looked at Patty and was like I am NOT going down from a bag of anti-nausea meds. I told the nurse that I hoped they were prepared if something did go wrong and she assured me they were, so onward we went. Of course, the power of suggestion ~ I felt every symptom you could imagine and I tried to busy myself so as not to create a problem where there wasn't one.

I made it through that bag and all four of the others. By now it was evening. I had completed my first chemo treatment and my body was full of the poison that we hoped would attack the monster and not just damage me.

I was unhooked from everything and I wandered out into the lobby. I was kind of scared to go home for fear something would happen to me. I felt very secure having Tom around and I hugged him and cried. I told him I was afraid. He assured me that if my body was going to have a severe reaction it most likely would have already done that. Tom and Patty offered to come home with us that night, but I said that I thought we would be ok and we would call them at any time if we needed them.

And so in the darkness of that December night Kevin and I headed back home. I got a hot shower and in God's great mercy I fell asleep for the whole night.

Pity
Party

About two days after the treatment I thought I might just curl up and that would be the end. Obviously there was a reason they called it the red devil of chemo. It was a poison like no other!! I experienced just about every side effect you could imagine.

One day at a time it got a little better. I had "to do" lists and on that list for the entire day would be ~ wash hair or get a shower or sit in a chair for a little.

One evening I had a complete meltdown. It was an ugly meltdown but a much needed meltdown. There is no way to measure the effects those drugs have on the mind and the emotions and the body and the spirit.

I got myself together and found a clean pair of jammies and landed on the couch just in time to hear the re-airing of Jimmy V's speech on ESPN in honor of his cancer foundation.

These are the words I heard ~

"Never give up ~ never, ever give up!! Cancer cannot take my spirit, my soul, my mind. Make sure you laugh every day...that you take time to really think...and that you let your emotions be moved to tears each day!!"

Wow ~ did I need to hear all of that at that very moment. I could find things to laugh about...I had plenty to think about...and there were plenty of tears too. I learned that if I could laugh and think and feel deeply each day ~ that would be a good day!! Cancer did not own me. Cancer did not define me. Each day that I endured and survived and fought was a check in the win column.

Control
Freak

One morning I found myself up in the wee hours of the morning. My appetite was slowly coming back and I decided to fix one scrambled egg and put a little green tea on ice. I nibbled and sipped and could taste nothing but hoped that it would give me some strength.

I sat with the Christmas tree lights on and got to thinking about the fact that I had always been a control freak. When my kids were little I had never let them decorate the tree because I wanted everything to be "just right". (major regret) This Christmas as I was facing death right in the face all the things that I thought mattered so much did not!! That December I started a new tradition and that was to have the grands decorate our tree each year for the rest of my life.

The evening that they came over Kevin brought up the boxes with the decorations in them and I sat on the couch. I literally did nothing but watch. Mr. Honey struggled a bit with my new carefree spirit because he really wanted those strands of beads hung just right, but as if I was pulling his teeth he backed off and let the kiddos do their thing.

Let me tell you ~ the tree never looked more beautiful!! Ok, so if you bumped the tree, random ornaments would fall off and you had to overlook the clusters of ornaments all on one branch. But I refused to move anything. It was perfect!!

I realized that morning that very few things that we fret and worry and fuss about are really worth all the stress. Being together...laughing...being imperfect...being simple...that's what actually mattered!!

Christmas
2017

"Occasionally weep deeply over the life you hoped would be ~ grieve the losses ~ then wash your face ~ trust God ~ and embrace the life you have"

Those were the words on the first page of the 2017 date book that I had bought. Little did I know how much I would need those words thru that year. In January our Aunt Moner went home to heaven. Not too long after that Kevin's whole identity was stolen and it tooks months to resolve all of that.

About a year and a half prior I had started sending out letters and reminders for the Palmer family Christmas at the lodge. Every single member of the family was planning to be there. Earlier that summer my dad had suffered two heart attacks and he had spent weeks in the hospital on life support and then recovering. We all felt the importance of making sure we were all together ~ first of all to celebrate Jesus ~

but also knowing how quickly life can be taken from us, we just all wanted to be together.

After my dad was getting stronger was when I was then diagnosed in the fall. I had my first treatment December 1st and my second one was to fall on the 22nd which meant I would be way too sick to travel to the cabin and be with everyone. So after all of my planning and efforts, and basically not giving anyone a choice about being there, it appeared I would be the one that would not get to be there.

Long story short ~ Dr. V realized the timing of it all and knew the importance of me being with my whole family, and so she moved my infusion till after Christmas. Imagine the joy as I got to call each of the families and let them know I would be there after all!!!

It was an amazing Christmas and we were ALL TOGETHER!! The one thing I will never forget was when everyone gathered around me in the fireplace room and they prayed for me. Asking God for complete healing...asking for strength to endure the fight...and asking that ultimately His will would be done. We knew without a doubt that God was able to heal me...we prayed that it would be pleasing to Him to do so here on this earth.

I'm Going
to be Bald!

As I mentioned earlier, the two things that were the hardest for me were telling the four grandkids that I had cancer and being bald. Chemo and radiation and surgery seemed manageable to me in some way, but I could not stand the thought of the children being uncomfortable around me or living life without hair.

About a week and a half after my first treatment I was home alone, and I simply scratched my head and came away with a cluster of hair. I froze. My heart sunk. I guess that even though Dr. V told me I would definitely lose my hair, I still clung to the hope that maybe it wouldn't fall out.

As I stood there frozen I was afraid to move for fear it would just start dropping on to the floor. Needless to say the next week or so was very dramatic and stressful as each day more and more hair came out. Because I had three times the normal amount of hair I was able to still look pretty normal ~ it was just much thinner.

One evening Kevin and I were in a store waiting to check out and I touched my head and had another whole cluster of hair in my hand and I didn't know where to go with the hair. It was then I knew that I would need to shave my head asap!!

We got home and I told Kevin that the next day after he left for work I would be shaving my head. I honestly felt like I was in space or something. The very thing I dreaded so much was now becoming a reality and there was no way out. I called my brother, Scott, and I cried and told him what I would have to do the next day. I told him I still had no clue how on earth I would do this and how I would be ok. He showed compassion and grace and mercy...he hurt with me. We then devised a plan together of how I would do it. He would be a text a way the whole time.

That night I barely slept. I wept a few times. I did not want to be bald. I had a ton of hair my whole life and I believe that somehow that was a security to me and it made me feel so vulnerable and exposed to think of being bald.

Kevin left for work. I got out of bed like a soldier and gathered all my gear. Scissors. Razor. A trashcan to put the initial hair in. And then I found one of my favorite songs and put it on auto play.

I stood there crying...holding the scissors. I finally

got up the courage to lift the first curls and cut them off as close to my head as possible. For a little while I just sobbed and cut. The trash can was full of my curls and my "security". Soon I began to have this feeling of control...of courage...of bravery...of strength. The crying stopped. It was time for the razor and I finished by shaving my head. When I was all done this amazing sense of peace flooded over me. The very thing I was sure I could not do I had just done. I sent Kevin and Scott each a text and told them I was all done and I was ok. Sustaining grace at its best!!!

That evening I met Kevin at the door when he came home from work and I had a turban on my head and my gold hoop earrings. He set his things down and just held me as we cried and held each other tight. That night I slept beside him with a bald head and in the morning I found a note from him saying that he thought he loved me even more.

I was able to do all things through Him!! Thank you dear Jesus!!

Some Humor

Let's see ~ where do I begin??!!

How about with giving me three days of steroids that pumped me all up...then cold turkey stopping and having me be as mean as a hornet. That happened with all six chemo treatments. At the same time I was sick, sick, sick. Mr. Honey was trying his best to figure out what on earth to do to help me. I would send him to the store to get things that maybe I would try to eat. Only to try and eat them and they tasted like adult aspirin and I was so nauseous. I would just hand it back and tell him to take it to Krista so I wouldn't even have to know it was in the house.

One day I called and called for him to come upstairs since I was in bed for days at a time. I told him I needed a Coke and I needed it fast. So he goes downstairs to get one out of the fridge and is gone forever. I'm saying "bad" words under my breath. Trying not to throw up. Wondering what on earth had happened. He finally comes in so proudly carrying the requested Coke. I asked what on earth had taken so long. He told me that as he passed through the living room something distracted him on tv. Ummmmm ~ that was NOT a good answer and it is a miracle we survived such experiences many times. Haha!!!

How about runny, crunchy, cold, mashed potatoes!! My mother's buttery creamy mashed potatoes were kind of appealing to me and I was blubbering to him that that's what I wanted to eat. He told me he could make them for me. He was sure he had this!!

Again, it seemed like two days passed but meekly he came into the room with a little bowl of crunchy, runny, cold, mashed potatoes. He sweetly said that he hoped they tasted good. I took a little bite and the huge tears ran down my face. I was so sick and so tired and so mean and so help-less. I called him back and asked if he could at least rewarm them for me. I then sat on the bed and quietly took one little bite at a time. Actually the flavor was good if you didn't mind the crunch and the runny.

One more thing ~ one of the drugs numbed my fingertips and I was not to touch anything cold or hot so as to prevent permanent nerve damage. I can't tell you how many times he brought me Italian ice to try and eat and he would just hand me the freezing cup. One other time he brought me something hot and I sat there wondering what I was to do with it.

My dear honey ~ thank you from the bottom of my heart for trying. I didn't even know how to take care of myself so no wonder you were clueless half the time. But you sure gave it your best shot!! Well, I still don't excuse the distraction with something on the tv thing!!!! Ha!!

PS ~ We did learn to buy already made mashed potatoes and when I could I ate them.

Last
Hard Chemo

The day had finally come. I was to have my last round of six hard chemo treatments. It also decided to snow like crazy that day. Normally snow is one of my most favorite things but this time not so much because Brad and his son Cade were flying in to celebrate with me. Kyle and his family were coming in also from Indiana. And Tom and Patty and Krista's family wanted to be at the hospital too that day.

Believe it or not, everyone made it in safely. What we did not realize was that while we were all in the hospital for hours, the snow continued to come down heavily and the rest of the world was shutting down.

The bags of drugs were finally all done and I was unhooked and everyone was wearing "Team Cheri" t-shirts and they were waiting at the bell for me to ring it in celebration. Nurses gathered around and I rang that bell as loud as I could and we all cheered. One huge step was now complete.

It was time to party. We all gathered our stuff and got our vehicles and started heading to where we were going to have supper and have our party. As we caravanned thru Hershey and Harrisburg we found that every single eating place was closed. And on top of all that one of the grands threw up in our van and that was for sure the end of our party mood. We all said our goodbyes in the parking lot of the mall. I tried not to cry. I had just been through the hardest months of my life and was so ready to celebrate and it just wasn't going to happen the way I pictured.

We got back to the house and Kevin cleaned up the van and I showered and then cuddled with Lowyn till I was ready to sleep.

I couldn't help but be thankful for so many things. I had made it through that awful chemo with almost no complications. My doctor already had the next steps of our attack planned out. The fight would go on but for that night I would close my eyes and sleep and count the blessings that God had so graciously given us.

An
Angel ????

This is a random sweet, sweet story that I couldn't miss sharing.

On one of my many trips to the medical center I had finished my appointments and Kevin was getting the car from valet. I wanted to take a Starbucks drink home to Krista because of the many times she had filled in the gaps and helped me when Kevin had to be working.

I got in a long line and was lost in thought as I was waiting my turn. I must have looked like a cancer patient because I could sense people checking to see what might be wrong with me. Obviously I was bald and had my little hat on. I probably looked a little weary. I was pretty sure they weren't checking me out cause I was so hot ~ haha ~ a hot mess ~ YES!!!

It came time for me to place my order and I was getting ready to pay. A man seemed to come out of nowhere and leaned over my shoulder and he handed his credit card to the cashier and told her to let me get anything that I wanted. Well just awwwwwww. I really didn't know what else to get so he paid and as I turned, with tears running down my face, to say thank you to him he was gone.

The entire area got very quiet. Many people had tears in their eyes. Many people gave me the warmest smiles. It was such a simple, sweet act of kindness and not only did it melt my heart and make me feel cared about and special in some way, but it also touched everyone around me.

I told Kevin all about it as soon as I got out to the car. I told him that it was as if an angel swooped in and God's love was shown to all of us there in that moment.

I'm pretty sure it was a real man just walking by with a heart full of kindness and God bless him. He will never know what he did for me that day. I still wish I could say thank you to him. I will never forget how I felt.

It made me want to be a better person. To be that kind of person. Seeing the hurting, and maybe not be able to fix it, but making them feel special and making them smile.

Maybe, just maybe, it really was an angel. It's fun to think it might have been. Thank you dear Jesus for loving us in such amazing ways.

Big
Decisions

Now that the initial six rounds of chemo were done it was time to move on to the next steps in this fight. I had an MRI and some other tests done and every one of them showed the chemo had done its job and the tumors were all gone. ALLLLLLL gone!!!

Now it was time to go back into the care of my surgeon and decide whether I would have a single or double mastectomy. Would I have any reconstruction??!!

First, I had to clear things with Christian Healthcare and they said anything we chose to do would be covered. That was a huge relief.

I also had some genetic testing done and all those tests came back normal which was a huge gift for my daughter and my granddaughters. There was nothing about my cancer that was hereditary and they were not at any more risk because of me. Another huge relief!!!!!!!!

I told my surgeon that I wanted a double and that I

did not prefer any reconstruction. Well, because it was such a huge decision in my life she said I had to consider every option and that I was to meet with a plastic surgeon first. I didn't want to, but at this point I knew she was looking out for me and didn't want me to have regrets down the road. Krista went with me and mostly I was just looking forward to the time with her and where we would get lunch afterwards.

Probably one of the most humiliating times in my life was this particular appointment. I will spare you most of the details...but I was told that if I didn't get reconstructive surgery, I would probably suffer depression, and feel less feminine, and that I would lose a lot of self confidence.

But see, for me, I knew that my worth and my value came from a far deeper place. That I truly wasn't defined by my body. I'm not saying that my decision would be right for every woman in this situation but I did know what I felt in my heart for me.

I had several days after that appointment to pray and to read all the literature before I would see my surgeon. I remember getting up the morning I was to see Dr. Paulishak again, and I sat on the bed and read the papers one more time and asked the Lord to show me if I was to consider anything else.

Kevin took me to the appointment and we rode in silence. Honestly it was daunting. Kevin had told me this was totally my decision and he was just going to be praying for me.

We arrived at the office and were taken back to the room. I still had not said out loud what I was going to do. Dr. Paulishak came in and as always I just loved spending time with her. She then asked what I had decided and I blurted out "a double with no cosmetic surgery". Peace I cannot explain poured into my heart and mind. You could see the peace on her face and on Kevin's. Very quickly she got things in order and the surgery date was picked and I was talking to other staff about all the details to get prepared.

It sounds crazy to say that I was excited, but I was. Is that God or what?? What I was facing was not something any woman would want to have to go through and yet peace and joy and contentment flooded my soul.

We finished all we needed to do that day at the office and we went out to the car and I started texting family members and friends ~ telling them the date of the surgery ~ as if I was telling them when my new baby was coming or something.

On a side note ~ I have never regretted the decisions

I made that day. I have never felt less of a woman. And Mr. Honey has never made me feel anything but beautiful to him.

Thank you again, dear Jesus, for taking something that would seem impossible and giving grace and strength and courage that could come from nowhere else but YOU. I love you for that!!!!!

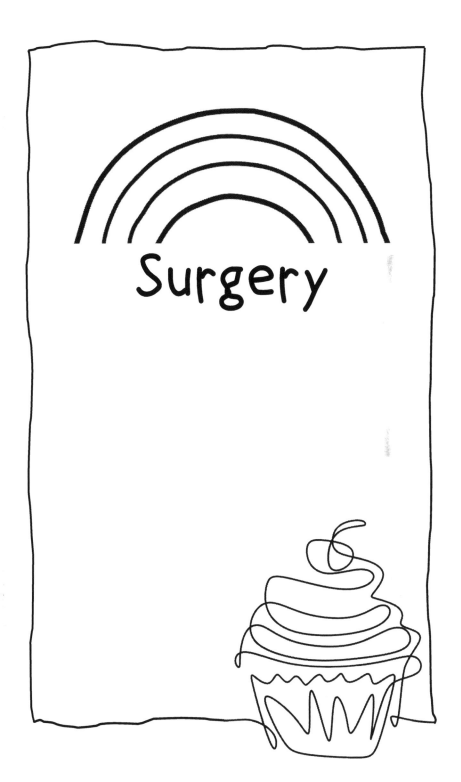

Surgery

The night before surgery Tom and Patty parked their truck and trailer at a nearby church so they could be close to me for about a week.

I slept peacefully that night ~ as if nothing unusual was going on at all. Woke up the next morning in good spirits and was ready to get this done. I went about my normal routine and I don't remember feeling anxious or nervous at all.

We met up with Tom and Patty and they followed us to Hershey very early that morning. When we got there I went through the procedures of getting checked in and then we headed to the pre-op area. I remember thinking to myself that I should be nervous or sad or feeling sick or something. But instead I was happy and full of peace and there must have been tons of grace surrounding me.

I got called back to my tiny little area where they would prep me for surgery and monitor me for awhile.

Kevin was with me. I met the anesthesiologist and an assistant to Dr. Paulishak. She even stopped by for a quick visit. All the while I was enjoying Altoids to keep my breath fresh and minty.

Of course, I wasn't to have anything to eat or drink since midnight the night before but I didn't think a mint counted as something to eat. It was close to surgery time and my team stopped by one more time and one of them noticed I had something in my mouth. When I told them it was just a mint everyone got quiet. They very kindly told me that was part of the do not eat rules and that my surgery would be postponed for a little while. They decided to go do another shorter surgery and told me no more mints!!!

In the meantime, Kyle and Kelly and Lowyn were able to make it over to the hospital from their home in Hershey and they were allowed to come back and see me. I was able to have Lowyn right on my bed with me till it was finally time for me to go. I'd say baby cuddles were probably the best thing for me right before major surgery.

Kevin was allowed to come along with me to a certain point as they pushed my bed through the big halls and down corridors. We finally stopped at a corner and they said it was time to say our goodbyes. Of course there were tears on both of our parts and we waved till we couldn't see each other anymore.

In just minutes I was wheeled into the big operating room and I remember thinking I was dreaming. It didn't look or seem real. They helped me on to the operating table and I remember telling them that now I felt afraid. They told me that was ok and they promised to take the best care of me and within minutes I was asleep. The surgery was a good four hours or more and then I was taken to a recovery area for quite a while.

I remember starting to wake up. I loved the feeling of the blood pressure cuff on my arm. I loved the sound of the machines. I loved the warm blankets. I did feel like an elephant was sitting on me. Eventually they took me to the room I would be staying in overnight. Kevin was the first to come see me and I do not remember that at all. Sorry honey!! I do remember seeing Tom and Patty for a few minutes. And then I had a little time with Kevin's mom and sister. I was not in any pain at all.

Eventually I became fully with it and I do remember everything from that point on including my honey. Things were pretty quiet until a nurse checked me and I was developing quite a nice hematoma near the incision. Within minutes people were flying around and before I knew what happened they had me wrapped tight in ace bandages to put as much pressure on it as possible to prevent any more swelling, or the need to go back to surgery.

That night Kevin and I spent one of the sweetest nights of our lives together. I was in my bed with the socks that massage your legs ~ amazing!! Kevin pulled a lounge chair right up beside my bed so we could hold hands. Three times that night he helped me across the hall to use the bathroom. He would help me get back in bed and make a nest of pillows all around me and he would hook up my cool socks and then he would get back in his chair and hold my hand. True love at its very best.

The next morning I was ready for breakfast. I had learned how to take care of my drains and they were planning to send me home before lunch. Tom and Patty came. I got dressed all by myself and signed all the discharge papers and got myself in a wheelchair and was ready to hit the road.

Once again Tom and Patty followed us, and this time we were heading back home. I rode along thinking to myself that I had arrived at the hospital with my body looking one way just the day before, and in a little over 24 hours I was leaving with my body totally different forever. I also remember thinking ~ I AM STILL ME!!! My body might have changed but I didn't. I was still a wife...a mother...an

Amma...a friend...a sister...a daughter...a Christian. None
of that was taken from me ~ and that was the stuff that
mattered to me.

I had a very uneventful recovery. Never had
pain. The drains were the most bothersome and pinched,
but overall I healed perfectly and without any complications.

It was time to check off another step in this fight!!!!!

Christian
Healthcare

I think this bit of information is too good not to share. It is kind of random right here in the middle of everything, but it's such an example of how God was working long before we even knew what we were facing.

The cost of medical insurance was out of control. The deductibles were terribly high. The company where Kevin works was offering an alternative plan called Christian Healthcare Ministries. It's a sharing program where Christians help pay for one another's bills. We had thought about it the year before and then chickened out, thinking we felt more secure with traditional insurance.

The year that I would be diagnosed we felt strongly that God wanted us to make the change and try the sharing program. We researched everything. Kevin figured all the numbers out. I could picture God having to be so patient. He knew all along this would be the best option considering what would be ahead of us with my health. It just took us a little extra time to catch on. Kevin and I aren't real big fans of change. Haha!!

We finally decided to go for it. I remember thinking that this isn't gonna work and someday we will probably lose everything. Not sure why the traditional insurance that cost a fortune felt more secure but I guess it was all we had known to that point.

Little did we know that the very thing that God wanted us to do would be the very thing that took care of every single medical bill, without even having to pay a deductible. Bills that we couldn't even wrap our minds around the amount, were all shared by other Christians.

God knew all along that if we had stayed with traditional insurance we would have had to pay a large deductible each year and all the copays plus the high monthly premiums.

It amazes me to look back and see that God was already working things out, and had things in place, ready to help us when our time of need came and when we would be facing years of huge medical bills.

Christian Healthcare has been amazing to work with. They pray for us. They check on us. We are put in contact with other families to pray for. We can send cards and notes of encouragement and I have received plenty myself.

Let me know if you ever want more information. I will gladly share!!!!! Or you can just go online and search Christian Healthcare Ministries.

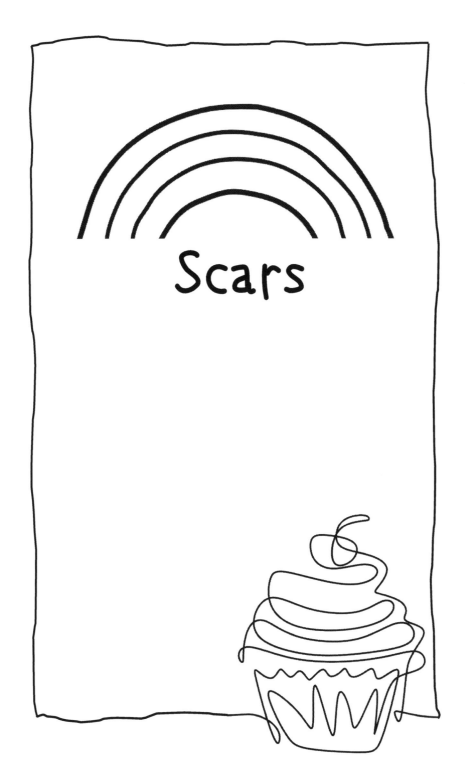

Scars

I love scars!! I really, really do. Scars tell stories and I love stories as you can tell!!!

My dad has a big scar on his one thigh and I remember as a little girl hearing him tell us the story of how he got that scar. He told us many times and it always ended with him getting the piece of bone out of his dresser drawer that had been removed from his leg.

Our son, Michael, has a scar on his stomach from being a preemie and having major surgery as an infant. I have always loved seeing that scar because it reminds me that three times in the first weeks of Michael's life God spared his life. It's a reminder of grace and mercy and the ones that did everything they could to help us.

And now I have a scar from underneath one armpit ~ all the way across my chest to under the other armpit. I remember the evening that Patty helped me remove all the bandages from my surgery. It was very sobering...we really didn't say much. She got the last of the bandages off and she left the room in tears and I sat there and cried for a while. And then I remember blowing my nose and wiping the tears and saying to myself that now this huge scar was a part of me and I was going to embrace it and love it. It would always remind me of how God carried me through the major storms.

You've maybe heard these words to a song before ~ "Heal the wound but leave the scar. A reflection of how merciful You are". God healed the wound but I'm glad He left the scar. My scar tells a big story and I don't ever want to forget.

I will tell you this ~ one day in radiation the big robot stopped right over me and I could see my chest in the reflection, with just this big scar. That day the tears ran out of my eyes, and into my ears, and down onto the table. I think it was one of those moments that the reality of it all hit me. But that was the only day I cried about how I now looked.

My friend, Bobbi, sent me this quote one day ~

"Maybe life isn't about avoiding the bruises. Maybe it's about collecting the scars to prove we showed up for it"

I can honestly say I love my scar. It is for sure a reflection of just how merciful He was. It somehow reminds me of how much He loves me. I know that humanly that might not sound logical...but I am telling you that I look down and I would not want to be without my scar now.

Dear God ~ thank you for healing the wound. Thank you for leaving the scar. xoxoxoxo

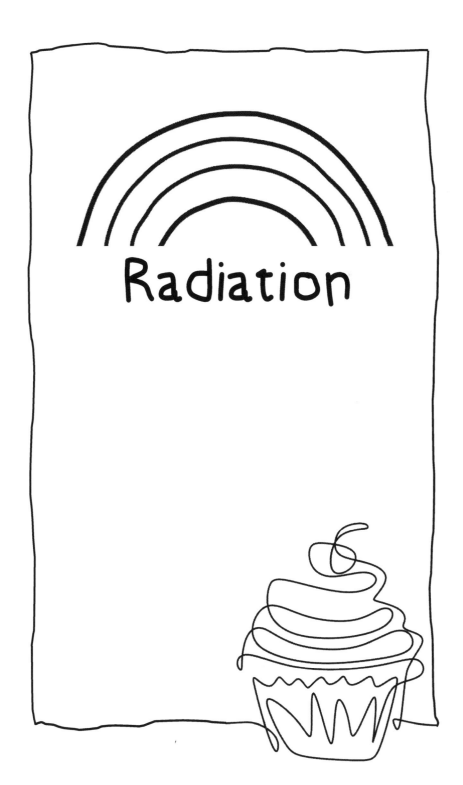

Radiation

We were now to the third stage in this first year of fighting. Hard chemo was done. Major surgery and recovery were done. All my pathology tests came back clear. They could not find cancer anywhere. Chemo had done its job and killed the rotten stuff.

I questioned why I would still need radiation, and they explained that they wanted to be as aggressive as possible because I had such an angry, active cancer that was growing and spreading fast when they found it.

I met Dr. Rosenberg ~ my radiation oncologist. Yet again God gave me just the right doctor for me. We went over everything and she decided that 30 rounds of radiation would be best for me. That would be five days a week for six weeks. We set up all the appointments. There would be a day to give me all my tattoos and mark me all up with black sharpies and put stickers all over me. Then I would come back for a practice run to make sure the computers and robots were all doing the right things. Then I would start my 30 days after that!!

One evening I was feeling completely overwhelmed with the weeks ahead of me and wondering how on earth I would ever be able to do all of that. I was also getting maintenance infusions every three weeks to keep fighting off cancer in hopes it would not come back ever, or at least not for a very long time.

My devotions that evening had these words ~ "I will give you everything you need to cope with the challenges you face. Don't waste energy projecting yourself into the future".

That was just what I needed to read and to be assured of again…He was always right there…promising everything we need for every need we have.

Everything was in order and it was time for my first day. I went to get in the car and sitting on the corner of the garage roof was a beautiful dove. Now in all the years we have lived in our home there has never been a dove there before that day and there has never been one since that day.

To me a dove represents peace and the presence of the Holy Spirit. All that I could think in that moment was that His presence was going to go with me and He would give me peace.

We got to the hospital and one of the first people to work with me, and to help me through the process of getting ready, was a man that literally reminded me of my brother, Scott. It was so comforting to be with someone that felt so familiar. He was kind and gracious and attentive and caring. When I left Kevin, to go down the hall I would go down many times, I was not afraid.

I got back to the waiting area and got my gowns and my locker and my key and got changed. I then went and sat in the waiting room till it was my turn. In the weeks to come I would meet some amazing people while we waited our turn to be radiated. One of which was my dear friend, Karen. We felt like best friends right from the start and she will be my forever friend. She is a Christian and we even have friends in common. Small world sometimes.

I handled radiation very well. My worst side effect was being so sleepy after the treatment. I would need good hearty food and a big nap and then I would be ok till the next round.

Some people are very anxious because of the machines and the fact that you are kind of suspended in the air as the robot goes around you and does its work. I am grateful that for that round of 30 treatments I was not afraid and I had theeeeee best techs one could ever hope for. It was just part of my life for a month and a half and we got into a good routine. I loved the week that my friend, Crystal, came in from Michigan and she gave Kevin a break and she took me to each treatment that week. Thank you my bestie. Being with you is always the best!!!!

The very last week the skin under my arm began to burn and blister. I was given an antibiotic ointment to put on it when the treatments were over to prevent infection while it healed. I went to several baseball games for the grands with a pillow under my arm to prevent any rubbing and that's how I sat in the bleachers. Sometimes you just do what you have to do when it comes to those grands. I never wanted to miss anything if it was possible for me to be there!!!!

On the last day of treatment Krista and the four kiddos came with flowers and treats for me and they got to watch me ring another bell ~ this time for the completion of 30 radiation treatments!!!!!!

God had done what He told me He would do ~ He gave me everything I needed to cope with that challenge and now it was also behind me!!!!!!!

Kindness

Here's just another little something random but seems worthy of telling. Kindness really does make a difference in our big world and in the day to day interactions we have with one another.

I have checked in to Hershey Medical Center more times than I can count. When you enter the Cancer Institute there is a whole area with people ready to check you in and give you all the paperwork you need for whatever reason you are there.

One day I stepped up to the window and the lady greeted me in a weary voice. I said hello to her and before long she was telling me that she hadn't had sleep for weeks because her back had been hurting from the chairs they have to sit on there at work. She went from one complaint to another and I stood there quietly and was kind and thoughtful.

Now mind you ~ for over a year I had to make a nest

to try to sleep in ~ had to learn to sleep on my back. I was either recovering from biopsies or sick, sick, sick from chemo or had drains coming out of me from surgery or had a raw armpit from radiation.

I stood there wanting to remind her that she was dealing with one cancer patient after another that could probably out-suffer her every single time. But I decided to try something different because I must have been having a good day. I thanked her for being there that day and for helping all of us get checked in because we needed every-one to do their job so we could fight cancer. She literally stopped what she was doing and looked up at me and she thanked me for caring. Sometimes a person just wants and needs to be heard and validated.

After that she treated me like we were best of friends and she wished me well and she was sorry for all I had to go through to fight cancer. I think that instead of telling her off, my choice to be kind to her made her feel better and quickly reminded her that most of us she was dealing with that day had it far worse then she did. I bet for the rest of the day it changed her outlook and she probably became a blessing to other patients.

Not going to lie ~ I was sure it would feel good to say something like "you do realize you are talking to a cancer patient and you are complaining about how hard your life is, right??!!!"

Kindness usually wins though, and on that day I was glad I heard her. Through the years I have tried very hard to be cheerful and kind to the nurses and doctors and techs and assistants. I have found that most times if I am kind and gentle they treat me really well and I have made some of the best friends there at the hospital. Only once or twice I wasn't able to break someone down and they treated me terribly but then again we don't always know what heavy burden they might be carrying.

And just to keep it real ~ I know there have been my times where I just was over it all and was a grumpy mess. It's just the reality of life!!!!!

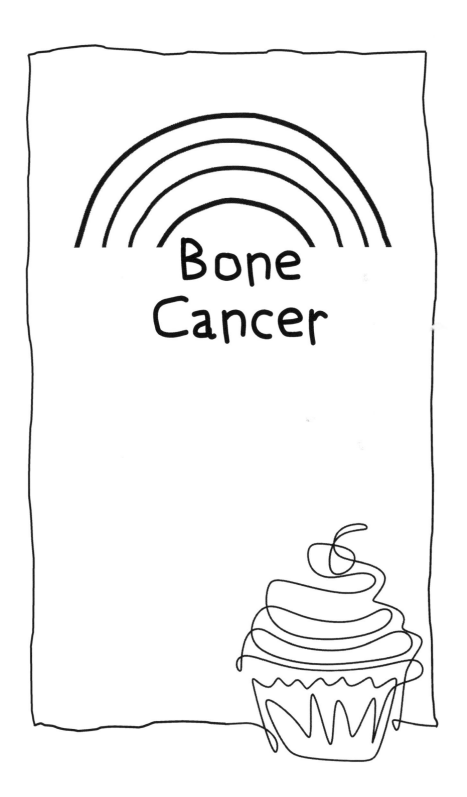

Bone
Cancer

I had done everything I was supposed to do. Six rounds of hard chemo. Continued maintenance infusions every three weeks. Surgery. Radiation.

I was feeling great and was enjoying life to the fullest. Shopping. Going places by myself which meant driving by myself too!!! Church. Out to eat. Small vacations. Games. Cooking and cleaning. Alllll the good stuff!!!

It was now time for my first bone and CT scans since all the hard work was over that we had done for a year. There really are no words to explain what it feels like to face those scans every three to four months. Every single time it all has to go back on the altar. My wishes and dreams and hopes all given back to Him in complete surrender that whatever those results would be I would trust Him.

Scan day came and I got the injection of dye into my bones. Then I went on to my chest and pelvic CT scans. Then back for the scan of the bones. It takes about four hours for the whole process.

"With my love and my sadness I come before you
Lord. My heart is in a thousand pieces. Maybe even
more. When all that I can sing is a broken hallelujah. When
my only offering is shattered praise. Still a song of adoration
will rise up from these ruins. I will worship you and give you
thanks. Even when my praise is a broken hallelujah."

The next morning, as I was alone, I got a call from
Dr. Vasekak ~ my oncologist. I could tell her heart was
hurting. We made a tiny bit of small talk but I knew what
she was going to tell me. They had found more cancer and it
was in my bone and was rather large. I didn't pass out...
I didn't scream...I didn't cry. I calmly asked her what this
meant for me because we had made a promise right from
the start to be totally honest. She said that in medical terms
I was now considered incurable. I asked her how long could
I possibly live. She told me good scenarios can be one to two
years depending on the drugs we used and how I responded
to them. I thanked her for telling me the truth. I then told
her that those numbers and statistics did not scare me because I knew my life was in God's hands and I knew that I
would not be going anywhere till it was exactly when God

planned for me to be going.

Please do not get me wrong. I did not want to die. It's not that Heaven and the thought of seeing Jesus aren't amazing, but it's the thought of leaving that always messes me up.

I asked her what our plan was, and she said we could try another drug and also she would talk to Dr. Rosenberg to see if five rounds of radiation on that bone was possible. I told her I was all in and was ready to start ASAP!! We hung up and we both were feeling emotional. We were both saddened that the cancer had acted up again so soon and we hated that we already had to devise a new plan to fight it off again!! Before we hung up she so sweetly asked me to ask my family to pray for her ~ that she would make the right decisions concerning my care. That's a special doctor right there!!!

I called Kevin first and just asked him to come home. When he got here I told him and the floodgates opened and we cried and cried. It was another one of those times that I was sure was not real. Like somehow I was on the outside of this bad dream looking in.

I then told our kids and of course we were all sad, but I asked them to remember that God still loved our family and that God was still a good God even when life was being cruel.

Then the only other thing I could think to do on that day was to go see my parents. We had lunch together ~ we prayed ~ we hugged ~ we cried ~ we gave it all to the Lord and I left ready to fight some more.

The new drug started to kill the cancer right away and the five rounds of radiation did their job too. Each time I would go for scans the area got smaller and smaller. During that time they found another suspicious spot on a rib and we zapped that with some radiation too. Over the next months those areas became non-measurable and I did not develop any new places.

"While our circumstances constantly change, God's faithfulness to see us through our circumstances ~ and even use them for His glory ~ never changes."

Bubbles

I was on the new infusion drug for quite a while and
it was doing a great job of killing the cancer in the bones,
and it was preventing any new cancer from appearing. But
over the months the drug started to become too strong for
me and it was breaking me down.

We went on a Pannebaker family (all 13 of us at that
time) vacation and I enjoyed every second to the fullest. It
was amazing to all be in one place and wake up each morning to five little kids calling my name as they came down the
hall, looking for my room. One morning I opened my door
and a lady wondered if I was Amma. She then told me that
earlier a tiny blond was going up and down the hall calling
for Amma. Well just awwwww!!

We rented a beautiful boat one afternoon and jet
skied and ate ice cream and swam in the lake and cooked on
the patio and played games late at night. As the week went
on, I could tell I was getting weaker, but I didn't let it stop

me from doing every single thing I could.

Just a couple days after our vacation I started to fall apart. I became very sick and could not eat. I was so weak I couldn't get out of bed. I lost 15 pounds in just a week or so. I literally thought my body had given up and I was dying.

We made several trips to the hospital to have fluids put in me because I was so dehydrated. Finally Dr. V ordered a trip to the ER and wanted all kinds of tests done on me. We found out that everything was ok and all the things they were looking for were negative.

One evening, during the time that I was so sick, I asked Kevin to sit on the back porch with me and just blow bubbles. It was the best I could come up with for a date. Bubbles make me happy and I sat there barely able to hold my head up, but I got lost in watching the bubbles float away.

I believe it was that night that I posted on Facebook that we had a bubble date. The next morning two different bubble machines were sent to my house by two very special people. One of the machines was damaged in the shipping and because two were sent God had made sure that I would still have one. O how I have loved my bubble machine.

Just a few days later I was at the hospital for fluids

and was waiting in the lobby to check in. I was holding a barf bag. I was so weak I could hardly stand. I was just plain sad and scared. Out of nowhere bubbles started drifting down by our heads and I looked at Kevin and we both had tears in our eyes. One of the volunteers at the hospital was standing at the balcony, right above us, and was blowing bubbles down just to spread cheer. That never had happened before that and it has never happened since.

Once again, I saw how much God loved me and how He wanted to make sure I knew He was right there. He knew I loved bubbles and He gave me some bubbles. AMAZING!!!

Thank the good Lord in time we decided to drop the infusion drug to the lowest dose possible and see if my body would be able to tolerate it. It worked and I started to gain strength back and was able to get back to a pretty normal life again.

Pink
Party

Michael and Brittany ~ our son and his wife ~ had a vacation planned to be at our house. It just happened to be during that time that I would hit a one year anniversary of not having any measurable cancer or any new cancer in my body.

A party was in order. After all, I had learned that we should celebrate every little thing. Every little victory. Every little step. So a pink party it was going to be!!!!

We had a big Palmer family group text going that day. Everyone was sharing how they were celebrating with us ~ long distance ~ with wearing pink or eating something special or wearing something special like the big gold hoops Kayna and I each had a pair of.

Gifts arrived in the mail. Gifts were delivered. There were gorgeous flowers and balloons...not the scary latex ones though. I'm allergic to latex and yet I still think my kids think I make that up. Haha!!

Everything was pink. Krista made amazing cupcakes that were decorated in every shade of pink. Tablecloths ~ spoons ~ cups ~ all pink!!!!!!!!

I was showered with love and spoiling. But mostly, I was humbled and thankful that God in His mercy had allowed me to be well and to still be here.

Did I say the word pink enough times in that story???!!!!

It was a special day. We even ran in the rain and just got soaked.

"Sometimes life isn't about waiting for the storm to pass. It's about learning to dance in the rain"

We laughed. We hugged. We celebrated.

Thank
You's

I was raised in a home where we were all taught to say thank you for everything. That has stuck with me my whole life and I am glad.

Here at the end of this little book I really wanted to write a chapter saying 'thank you' for so many different things. The only reason I hesitate to write this chapter is I am so afraid I will forget someone or something that deserves to be recognized. Sooooooo, if I do miss something or someone I promise I will write another book just so I can say thank you to you in a public way. Ok??!!

Very first ~ to Jesus ~ thank you for taking such good care of me. I love you and understand you more now then I did three years ago. I have had to endure and go through some pretty tough stuff...and you've always made a way. I cannot wait to see Your sweet face someday and have You reach down and take my hand and welcome me to Heaven. xoxo

Julie ~ the very first week that we were aware there was something wrong you sent me my first gift. And you have continued to shower me with gifts, of all kinds, for three years. Thank you for being so thoughtful and generous and caring. God has blessed you with the gift of giving and I know I am not the only one that has benefited from your generosity. I love you forever. I am reminded daily of your kindness as I see your gifts all through our home. xoxo

Kyle and Kelly ~ thank you for moving back to PA after I was diagnosed. When Kelly first told me that you guys were going to do everything possible to make it happen I honestly did not think it could or would happen. Little did we know that God already had the plan in place, and the transition happened so smoothly, and you moved just minutes from my hospital. You will never know how many times I have driven by your home after a long day at the hospital, and just seeing your home has brought comfort and courage. Many times I have sat in the hospital and just knowing you were minutes away helped me through. I loved the times Kyle showed up before a biopsy or a major test with a bouquet of flowers and a hug. Or the times Kelly brought Lowyn to see me during an infusion. Thank you for knowing that it mattered and for being close these past years. Oooooo, and I have to also say thank you for adding a new baby recently, because for me, there is no better medicine than a baby to hold. xoxo

Krista and family ~ thank you for painted rocks and pictures and cards and notes. For meals and other snacks and treats as the cravings came and went. For coming to many of my infusions and keeping me company. For being there to celebrate the big stuff like finishing six hard rounds of chemo and 30 radiation treatments. Colten, Alex, Cameron and Reverie ~ you will never know how much you have motivated me to fight this disease. You mean everything to me and I fought and will continue to fight because I don't wanna miss any part of your lives. xoxo

Michael and Brittany ~ thank you for my pink party and for all the fun we had that weekend celebrating the good stuff. Thank you for praying for me faithfully!! Thank you for going to the hospital with me one time while you were visiting so you could meet my doctors and see where I do what I do!! xoxo

Tom and Patty ~ thank you for coming to so many infusions and appointments at the hospital. For staying close by as I recovered from surgery. For the many treats and gifts and for all the love and support and compassion. I have always known you would be there for me if I needed you. That's a very comforting thought. xoxo

Brad ~ thank you for showing me how to fight this monster. You have always been my hero. Thank you for coming to one of my big appointments. For being there when I finished the six rounds of hard chemo. For making t-shirts for everyone to wear that day as we celebrated and I got to ring the bell. For talking me through the rough times when I needed someone to understand and listen and encourage. Thank you for challenging me in the right ways when I would get lost!! xoxo

Scott ~ thank you for the many times you have made me laugh. Thank you for coming to a couple of my appointments. Thank you for making sure I've always known you are right there to laugh or to cry with. To have deep talks or just be silly. You get me ~ you have always heard me and validated anything I have thought or felt. And you were the one that helped me shave me head from hundreds of miles away!! xoxo

Our parents ~ thank you for praying and praying and praying. For the hugs and the tears and the times we've laughed. Thank you for making coming to visit you feel so safe and normal. Thank you for the soups and meals and cards and notes and texts to constantly encourage and support. I know it has been very hard on all three of you at times, but you have always helped us keep the faith and

have reminded us over and over that God always has a plan
and doesn't make mistakes or waste our suffering. xoxo

Kim ~ thank you for the many gifts and for the times
you have taken a turn to give Kevin a break and have taken
me to all day appointments and meetings at the hospital.
Thank you for letting me know how much you love me. Oh,
and for letting me wear your gorgeous ring for all my hard
chemo treatments. You know it's a favorite of mine. xoxo

Crystal ~ thank you for the beautiful pottery you
made for me. And for the two beautiful dolls you gave to
me...they have been therapy and you knew they would
be. Thank you for coming for a week during chemo and for
coming for a week during radiation and for taking me to
treatments to give Kevin a break. I cherish the memories we
added during those weeks!! xoxo

Dr. Vasekar ~ Dr. Paulishak ~ Dr. Rosenberg ~ Dr.
Adams ~ Dr. Link ~ Dr. Noone ~ thank you for taking such
good care of me for all these years. Thank you for making
me feel like I matter. It comforts me to know that no matter
what is ahead in the days to come I know I have you and you
will continue to care for me and do what is best for
me. Many, many people have prayed for you, asking God to
give you wisdom as you have made many decisions about
my treatments. You are amazing doctors!! xoxo

Emily ~ first my radiation nurse and then my lab and infusion nurse. You have become such a special friend. I know my port sure has given you a rough time and you've always been so patient and kind. Thank you for taking time to listen. To give me pep talks. To talk about just normal stuff in life like our families. Thank you for genuinely being happy to see me and making me feel loved and cared about. I'll never forget the time we hugged without thinking during the pandemic. You truly are my forever friend and I will be thankful for you always!! xoxo

Gretchen ~ Andrea ~ Tammy ~ Ellie ~ Bobbi ~ Cindy ~ you each have gifted me with such unique gifts and plenty of cards and notes. Thank you!! But even more than that I know you have prayed so faithfully. You girls helped create the diva that thinks there should be packages on the front porch daily. Haha!! xoxo

Mr. Honey ~ I honestly do not even know where to begin in saying thank you to you. We've done it all together haven't we, honey! The good and the bad and the ugly and the sad. Cancer has been cruel and mean and it is hard on a marriage and a relationship but we always hold on to each other and fight through. I love you with my whole heart. I don't ever want to leave you. If I have any say I won't leave you, ok?!! For now I will just say a big thank you for everything. The beautiful jewelry gifts. The trips to the lake and ocean. For all the times you've told me I could have anything I want. For all the unlovely things you have had to help me with that no one knows about or sees...thank you!! You are my best husband and I will love you forever and for always. You and me!! xoxo

Prayers ~ thank you to the hundreds of you that have prayed so faithfully for sooooo long. It's been a long time to keep praying about the same thing and you have done it day after day. I know of someone that prays for me as soon as her eyes open in the morning and I know of someone who prays for me the last thing before she closes her eyes at night. Bless all of you. I cannot even say thank you enough or begin to tell you what it all means to me. xoxo

A huge thank you to the ones that have already given money to help with the printing of this book. I hadn't even thought that far ahead and money gifts were already being given. Bless you!! Big hugs!! xoxo

Lynn and Kim ~ thank you for having two fundraisers to raise money for gift cards so we could use them for gas and food and groceries during the six weeks of radiation, when we were exhausted and Kevin was working full time, and yet still getting me to all my appointments.

The stack of cards was wonderful and helped us day after day. And thank you, Lynn, for the summer I got so sick and you made me tons of homemade meals for my freezer and when I had zero strength to make anything to eat I just had to warm a good meal. And one more thing ~ thank you for making sure I have a Starbucks card for every infusion day. Those pink drinks bring a smile to the face! Loves!! xoxo

For all you athletes that ran races and marathons, and played "dig pink" volleyball, and hit home runs and wore pink for me. For a high school basketball team that won their game the night of one of my scans. For Alex and Cameron having their best hits in baseball and coming and telling me that was for me ~ THANK YOU!!!!!! You will never know how honored and loved I felt. I have some of your medals and ribbons and t-shirts and signed balls. Treasures I cherish!! xoxo

Pam ~ thank you for writing down almost every single post I have made on Facebook in the past three years. And also to Betty Lou, for printing many of the posts for me. I'm so grateful to have them for myself and for my family. They also played a big part in me being able to write these short stories because I had so many notes to look at. xoxo

Pam ~ thank you for taking care of what little hair I have been able to grow back. Most people get thick, curly hair after chemo and I had that before chemo and since then have had thin, fine- not curly hair. But you have taken good care of it and I am so grateful. Not to mention the days you come to cut my hair are the most fun just because we laugh and talk non-stop!! xoxo

Ingrid and Tanya and Ashley and Jan ~ thank you for always being ready to text at any time. I could tell you anything ~ whether good or bad ~ and you didn't judge my mood or attitude. I think there have been times that Tanya and I texted every night and that helped me so much when it got dark and the fears would roll in. Or maybe some nights there was something really fun to tell. There are many others of you that have been great companions thru texting and I am so grateful for that. It's amazing how just a simple text of love and care can change the whole way we feel, or whether we can just close our eyes and sleep peacefully because of some comforting words. xoxo

This is the longest chapter in this book but rightfully so. Without all of you ~ whether specifically mentioned or not ~ I could not do what I have to do. The support of family and friends is key in how the patient handles the huge challenges in this fight. YOU ALL have made a difference and I love you for it. Thank you to every single one of you that has made a comment on a post. Sent a text out of the blue. Sent a card in the mail. Brought a meal to us. Said a prayer. The hugs ~ oooo the hugs ~ they fill me right up!! xoxo

I have been blessed beyond my share with the best of family and friends and neighbors and medical staff!!

THANK YOU!! THANK YOU!!!

In
Conclusion

This seems like a very fitting time to be ending this book. Right now I am on an 11 week break from appointments and maintenance infusions. For three years I have been getting an infusion every three weeks. Probably isn't hard to understand that mentally, physically and emotionally I was so weary. Especially with adding the virus in the mix these past eight months. I had gotten to the place where I felt like I was carrying an elephant around. I was so sleepy all the time. I really wasn't doing much of a normal life. I had fallen a number of times because my joints and tendons were all so tight and damaged from the drugs.

We finally talked with Dr. V and we all decided a break was necessary to let me rest and rebuild and gain back the desire to keep in the fight. You see, I'm considered stage four and incurable, and so basically infusions to keep the cancer from coming back or spreading has been our goal now for almost two years. But when you get to the point that you feel like you don't care anymore, that's not good, because so much of the success in fighting this disease is a positive, uplifted spirit.

These 11 weeks have been so good for me. I have gotten to enjoy our new grandson ~ Ledger!! Have gotten to finish this book with a clear mind. Traveled. Been able to cook and clean and do laundry in a more normal fashion. Gotten to exercise and be out in the fresh air with Ellie, our wonderful neighbor, when we took a walk one morning. Haven't needed to use my cane as much. I feel strong and healthy again. I needed a reset button and this has really worked.

Two weeks from today it will be time to head back to Hershey for all my scans and tests and they will be looking for the cancer monster again. I don't feel like there is anything wrong with me but I also didn't know the other times either. But let's just say there isn't anything concerning me that would make me think it's back. Dr.V also has an infusion scheduled for late that afternoon to get back to fighting even if the scans are all clear.

Trust me ~ I do not want another scan or test. I don't want to have cancer anymore. I wish I could be excused now!! Daily I find myself having to give it all back to God. I want to live. I want to do a million more things

with Kevin. I want to spend more time with my kids and
their families. I want to see Reverie and Lowyn in their
wedding gowns someday. I want to listen to all the boys tell
me about the girls that have caught their eye. I want to see
more home runs and I long for more family vacations at the
lake and on and on.............

I pray, along with you, that God will heal me here on
this earth and never allow cancer to show up again. He
certainly is completely able to do that. The word incurable
is nothing to Him. I pray for what I desire and hope for ~
I tell Him I know He can do it ~ and then I surrender by
saying that I want His will to be done.

Just like He prayed to His Father before the crucifix-
ion. He asked that it could be removed from Him, but He
ended His prayer the same way I do ~ whatever was pleasing to God was what He wanted and that is what I want too.

One way or another, God is going to heal me. It will
either be here on this earth or it will be in His presence
when He calls me home. Humanly, I want it to be here on
this earth so I can have more time with all the ones I love. I
have some new goals and dreams that I would just love to
experience here on this earth.

But if cancer truly is the cause of my death someday,
and I go home to Heaven ~ well that is not a loss or a bad

thing. I will see Jesus!! That's a win all the way around!!

I want you to have that assurance too. I want you to know for sure that when your time comes to leave this earth you will be going home to Jesus forever!! If you do not know that, will you please reach out to me or will you please find someone that can point you to Jesus. At the end of the day He is truly all that matters. It's the most important decision of your entire life!!

If there was just one truth that you would always remember after reading this book of little short stories it would be this ~ that no matter what ~ God is good. If I go back in a couple weeks and they find more cancer He is still good simply by character and by definition. His goodness is not based on circumstances. If God chooses not to heal me on this earth...it's not because we didn't pray hard enough or we didn't have enough faith or that He didn't answer our prayers. It's simply because it was His perfect will to take me home and to heal me there. You will be able to REJOICE that God DID answer all of our prayers and He did it in the way that pleased Him!!

I sure am praying for clear scans. But if I have a new battle on my hands I will be refreshed and ready to fight again. I will give it all I have and I will draw from these stories to remember that He is real. He never leaves us or forsakes us.   He will give us all we need for every need we have.

This is the line I want you to never forget ~ no matter what happens in my life ~ no matter what happens in your life ~

AND IF NOT ~ HE IS STILL GOOD!!